THE LONG FAULT

THE LONG FAULT

poems

Jay Rogoff

LOUISIANA STATE UNIVERSITY PRESS
BATON ROUGE

Published by Louisiana State University Press
Copyright © 2008 by Jay Rogoff
All rights reserved
Manufactured in the United States of America
First printing

Designer: Michelle A. Neustrom
Typeface: MrsEaves
Printer and binder: Thomson-Shore, Inc.

LIBRARY OF CONGRESS CATALOGING-IN-PUBLICATION DATA

Rogoff, Jay.
 The long fault : poems / Jay Rogoff.
    p. cm.
 ISBN-13: 978-0-8071-3303-3 (alk. paper)
 ISBN-13: 978-0-8071-3304-0 (pbk. : alk. paper)
 I. Title.
 PS3568.O486L66 2008
 811'.54—dc22
                              2007019760

Many thanks to the editors of the following publications, where most of these poems appeared previously, some in different form: *Agni*: "The Guy Who Passed Me Doing 90 MPH and Playing the Trumpet"; *Hotel Amerika*: "Aspirations" and "Bar Mitzvah in Prague"; *Kenyon Review*: "Sublimated"; *Margie*: "Fifteen" and "In Camera"; *Notre Dame Review*: "The Golden Chamber," "In Hiding," "Just Say the Word," "Looking Out," and "Shadow"; *Partisan Review*: "Captivity in Spring"; *Prairie Schooner*: "Iconography" and "A Snapshot Is a Moment's Monument"; *Peregrine*: "Memorial Chapel" and "Mennonites by the Sea"; *The Progressive*: "Book Burning," "Folding the Flag," "The Hildesheim Doors," and "Memorial Chapel"; *Rattapallax*: "Flopping the Negative"; *Salmagundi*: "Flemish Adorations" and "Jane Austen, Inventor of Baseball"; *Shenandoah*: "Cain's Gift"; *Southern Poetry Review*: "Mysteries" and "Poets' Park, Mexico DF"; *Southern Review*: "Absorption," "A Breakdown," "Carmelite Convent, Mexico DF," "Ixcuintli," "Mennonites by the Sea," "Nether Stowey," "The Shield of Aeneas," "Still Life," and "Such Stuff"; *Western Humanities Review*: "Chawton," "Donne's Effigy," "A Fine and Public Place," and "The Glass of Fashion and the Mold of Form"; and *Witness*: "Pyramid of the Sun."

 "Mysteries" was reprinted in *Southern Poetry Review*'s fiftieth anniversary anthology. "Captivity in Spring" also appeared online at *Poetry Daily*.

 Excerpt from "As I Walked Out One Evening," in *Collected Poems* by W. H. Auden, copyright © 1940 and renewed 1968 by W. H. Auden, reprinted by permission of Random House, Inc., and Faber and Faber, Ltd.

 Excerpt from "The River-Merchant's Wife: A Letter," in *Personae* by Ezra Pound, copyright © 1926 by Ezra Pound, reprinted by permission of New Directions Publishing Corp.

 I am grateful to the Corporation of Yaddo for residencies during which many of these poems first came into being or found their final shape.

 I am also indebted to Skidmore College's faculty development committee for its generous support.

 I owe special thanks to editors whose support and suggestions made a difference: John Easterly, Richard Howard, Bret Lott, James Olney, and Matthew Rothschild.

 For advice and encouragement about some of these poems I am indebted to Terry Diggory, Rachel Hadas, Andrew Hudgins, Penny Jolly, Amelia Rosner, and Steve Stern, beloved friends all.

The paper in this book meets the guidelines for permanence and durability of the Committee on Production Guidelines for Book Longevity of the Council on Library Resources. ∞

For Penny

I desired my dust to be mingled with yours
Forever and forever and forever.

"The glacier knocks in the cupboard,
　　The desert sighs in the bed,
And the crack in the tea-cup opens
　　A lane to the land of the dead. . . ."

　　　　　　　　　　　　W. H. AUDEN

Contents

1. IN TIME
   Cain's Gift 3
   Iphigenia 4
   Sublimated 5
   Book Burning 6
   The Shield of Aeneas 9
   Aspirations 12
   Folding the Flag 13
   Donne's Effigy 14
   The Glass of Fashion and the Mold of Form 15
   A Fine and Public Place 16
   Pyramid of the Sun 17
   Ixcuintli 18
   The Guy Who Passed Me Doing 90 MPH and
      Playing the Trumpet 20
   Tempera 21

2. IN CAMERA
   Mysteries 25
   Flopping the Negative 27
   Flemish Adorations 29
   Looking Out 30
   A Snapshot Is a Moment's Monument 32
   Fifteen 33
   Shadow 35
   Captivity in Spring 37
   Nether Stowey 38
   Jane Austen, Inventor of Baseball 39
   Chawton 40
   Absorption 41
   In Hiding 42
   Iconography 44
   Adoration 45
   Just Say the Word 46
   Still Life 48
   In Camera 50
   The Golden Chamber 52

3. INEVITABLE

Mennonites by the Sea   57
A Breakdown   58
Such Stuff   59
Death's Suit   61
The Collapse   63
Bar Mitzvah in Prague   64
Carmelite Convent, Mexico DF   65
Memorial Chapel   67
The Hildesheim Doors   69
Three Women   71
The Old and New Cemeteries   73
Poets' Park, Mexico DF   76

I
IN TIME

CAIN'S GIFT

The blood cried up from the ground
and the air held its breath,
the earth's sunset-stained
face now an epitaph
for Abel's head and hands
thrust up from the grave,
that childish face profiled,
those hands clasped, a child

imagined by the sculptor
petitioning the God
who'd let the model murder
play out unimpeded.
From brother to his keeper
the singing from the sod
rose, a sunset lark
whose quavers left their mark

on Cain's consciousness,
setting him aquiver
at walking the cooling face
of earth, banished forever
from Salisbury's Chapter House,
a period put to his chapter,
and from the good book hurled
out to beget the world.

IPHIGENIA

Because the ocean wasn't turbulent,
because it stretched reflective as a summer
highway out to the classical horizon,
her shrieks across the windless sky thrilled them,
echoing off their clanging battle-skins
as they danced. Dark stains on her chiton spread
over her young topography, moist maps
of rising islands. A moister puddle swelled
around her naked feet, a vintage bitter
with terror, trickling from a source under
the dull knife-pleats damping her shivering thighs
and dribbling off the outcurve of her calves,
a stinking gold nectar they would have gargled—
hell, they'd have drunk her blood to sail to war,
to seduce wind to rise, ocean to roar,
small sacrifice when slaughter's bedroom eyes
beckon over the edge of the horizon.
Hallucinations flash in the Aegean
sun, any sun: the thought of Helen's hair
or secret weapons, holy oil and missions
tuning the world to sacred harmonies
like a soprano tearing the atmosphere,
strung tightly as a mortal voice can stretch.

SUBLIMATED

Fog rising from fallen snow
overleaps the liquid state.
That's how I would like to die,
raptured from gross solidity,
a subject saved from predicate
the way a single contrail splits
in seven in the barely blue
of barely air: the shuttle crew,
evading intervening states.

We aim so high because we're low,
citizens of gravity
collating wreckage that can't soothe
lovers at the grave. Low
flags mark our sublimity
while higher reaches thrum our nerves
as if, in the flaring scratch
of a phosphorus-perfumed match,
some human element survives.

BOOK BURNING

Fire loves paper
but adores people.
Fire eats our words,
hurling them off
like flaming birds
on bright black wings.
Smoke must cough
but fire sings,
breathing deeper,
sucking down
our oxygen.
Fire is not
our brother's keeper.
It isn't a question
of good and evil;
it guzzles the broth,
consumes the table.
Heine guessed
a modern truth:
they burn books first.

The night of the fire
on Unter den Linden
what rang up the curtain
next door at the Staatsoper?
Die Zauberflöte,
its gorgeous noise
lit with love,
a book of seduction,
light, and learning;
we walk through flame,
daring hell and high water,
dancing and burning,
our fancy fired up
till real tears drop.
Or *Tristan und Isolde,*
romantic hell

on a Celtic ship,
love mating death
till both look the same;
fire crests the wave
of the blood-dark ocean,
extinguished breath
blood-wet with kisses:
lovers, poison,
and none left to blame.

On the Opernplatz
the students wave
a sea of dark arms
engaged by armbands
and oozing the spume
of cream-pale hands
awash in the air.
Goebbels commends
their courage to break
the intellectual
reich of the Jew
and homosexual
and face the blaze,
courage to erect
in this vast empty platz,
banal and funereal,
a tower of books
and feed them to fire
like so many faggots.
The boys pledge death
divinest respect
with courage to burn,
courage to burn
Freud and all joy,
such men as Mann,
heretic Einstein,
and Heine the Jew.

The opera disgorges
its lovers, their eyes
still moist, songs still
in their teeth. They view
the night turned day,
the spring turned hell
this early May night.
The spines crack.
The burning covers
issue a smell
like living leather,
rank with authors.
Kerchiefs mask noses
and hands shield eyes
raised to the skies.

Another decade
and they'll take burning
to the very Beginning,
the primal Word,
spinning the world
back down the commode,
back into its Chaos
of mud and scheiss.
For now, bringing brightness,
words of all people
soar in a tower,
the babble of languages
melting together,
the fire-breathing steeple
drunk on air
and publishing ash,
singing like mad
a single song
in a single tongue.

THE SHIELD OF AENEAS

He sees the future twice,
once in, once back from hell,
peering out from Virgil
as from a yearbook, the war years,

the clean-cut high school hero
gone to soldier, fierce
anthems in his ears
drowning the tears of Dido,

waggling his wand at ghosts,
gladly sacrificing
all loved ones to slow singing
and blood-thick mists

parodying air,
an atmosphere with a sting
like ammonia on the tongue
and a smell like burning hair.

His buried father, standing,
stammers the dead words forth
from a chest bereft of breath,
bloody lungs gargling.

Aeneas's ears unravel
the next ten centuries,
unspinning like graveclothes
the yarns of an unborn people

played on a crazy loom.
They knit his brow, glaze his eye,
and echo in his hollow
heart, a fever dream

of wolves and Caesars,
an unenacted shade-tale

to hoist his sheet-white sail.
Later, when this future stares

him down once more he stands
stock stupid—
well, whose destiny wouldn't
harden one to bronze?

The hammered shield mirrors
the warring world his dutiful
and brutal beauty will
make necessary. He adores

the burnished slaughter,
parades and triumphs, nations
of heros, slaves, assassins
alloyed into empire:

but the bold Roman legend
that in the underworld
Aeneas heard unfurled
now knocks him ignorant

and thick as mortality,
obtuser than his readers.
Down among the shadows,
at the shade of a cypress tree

we can imagine Virgil
shrugging off his armor
a moment, like Homer's Hector.
This proud, imperial

contraption, the *Aeneid,*
soldered with politics
and greasy with flux,
he'd love us to assay it

in mute rapture—the shield,
this murderous, breathing metal,
incomprehensible
yet so well-smithed a child

could admire its articulate splendor:
Aeneas's stunning plunder,
the consummate brazen future
he hefts upon his shoulder.

ASPIRATIONS

But really, it's enough to make you gasp,
this gambling, this dicing with the world
order as in a game of Risk,
calm, murderous words like the rasp
of a bastard on a marble obelisk,
filing history to sand, polishing it bald
as a missile whose aspiration
to join the company of saints in heaven

comes crashing on the neighborhood of Eden.
We always want to think we're something more.
The woman longs to be a god, the man
to be in love. The serpent's subtler,
rehearsing to be master of all matter.
We dream we all own souls, sucked in like air,
and that aspirates huffing along the palate
and fricatives tickling the teeth are spirit.

As I lay on the operating table
naked under the childish laundered gown,
awaiting the needle's sucking of my fluid,
I rose to an unpinioned aspiration:
to keep intact my bundle of meat and blood
for touching, scribbling, loving, nothing an angel
could fall for, no inhuman appetite
for slaughter under cover of bearing light.

FOLDING THE FLAG

With a lover or friend
stretch it out waist-height
and parallel to the ground.
Fold lengthwise so blue midnight

and its strict constellation
vanishes under pure white
and blood red, a frisson
along the stripes, shot

between you. Fold again
lengthwise, a lot like unmaking
a bed in which no one
is ever just sleeping.

The stars should stay outside
as in the universe.
From the stripy end, fold
it up in small triangles,

kissing when you meet.
Tuck in the end, creating
a cocked newspaper hat
from whole cloth, a thing

useful in comforting
a suddenly public wife
suddenly veiled, her gold ring
shining like eternal life,

like moist eyes, like the bright stars
in her jaunty souvenir cap,
the weight of their universe
pressing into her lap.

DONNE'S EFFIGY

    Shelley's heart would not burn
    but here you stand entire,
  survivor of London's Great Fire,
rising erect from a scorched marble urn
        in effigy
  to reassure us we will suffer
combustion: God's wrath, lovers' holy scorn.
You stonewall both with equanimity

    to plunk saints on their knees,
    your stoicism, spread
  from pointed beard to broad forehead,
betraying none of the anxieties
      the Holy Sonnets
  dramatize, screaming for deathbed
lightbulbs, a glimmer of some final prize
to cramp those knife-breath last hours into minutes.

    The marble shroud coiled round
    your subtle, scrawny corpse
  tightens over the knees' round knobs
and caresses your spindly arms. Your left hand
      fondles your crotch—
  still the rake under divine wraps,
ogling virginal visions, though stone blind,
and smirking nakedly upon your church

    where, till your marble statue
    crumbles to dust again,
  no hand can chafe insurgent bone,
no gravedigger unearth in some far future
      a hair-braid bracelet;
  no laurels but a chilly crown
of fire, all passionate aromas burnt to
stone flame on your head, stone flame underfoot.

THE GLASS OF FASHION AND THE MOLD OF FORM

> Sidney is dead, dead is my friend, dead is the world's delight.
> FULKE GREVILLE

The flowers madly pollinate the room,
no bees to pander. On the wall once hung
the shaving mirror, now emptied of its face
and cut to this fragment, this fossil wing,
a flightless thing in which I loom concave,
monstrous and bald, badly needing a shave.
Sidney, though pampered from birth in this great house,
held his own razor, scraped the flame-red bloom
off his own chin, staring into this gloom
of dark glass where my eyes imagine his,
flashing, unnerving. I stick out my tongue.
Sweep the spilled pollen, set fire to the broom
and light the state cortège's slow progress,
a train so long the funeral engraving
from February 1587
sold in thirty-four separate images.
The men cast eyes about, at sea among
their fellow mourners, bewildered and stung
by that musket ball trailing its black perfume
and lodging in his leg. Sidney was young
no more, a shattered glass, a moldy bloom,
his luscious lines constructing a grand tomb
from our homemade English vernacular,
which he bragged best for verse of any tongue.
Turning to England, unmused in the earth,
he'd never know a decade later Shakespeare
would animate raw clay with English breath
and fire this hypothesis into truth.
Bid the riderless horse follow the groom,
brandish his empty helmet to worry Death:
let its device, the porcupine, assume
attack stance: upstart quills and stuck-out tongue.

A FINE AND PUBLIC PLACE

> But none, I think, do there embrace.

Everything about your grave's ironic,
that you, who hymned retirement and retreat,
turning gardens in turns of mind and phrase
as subtle as the signaling of fireflies,
should lie not in green shade but under pavement
in an urban church snug in London traffic.

How have you wound up London's and not Hull's,
your complaints hushed by the Thames, far from Humber?
How could that wingèd chariot lay out
a man who always landed on his feet,
first-in-command to Milton, later Member
who saved the blind man's bacon under Charles?

In the dark church, it's quiet as a blink
by your plaque, this embraceless country house,
your last retreat. Many of us would deal
the lush world for the privacy to scrawl
your most audaciously understated phrase
mocking our mocking steely Death: *I think.*

PYRAMID OF THE SUN

You're bringing your father back—not from the grave
but the years-long granite acquiescence
of Alzheimer's, and from the liquid silence
of decades before. You want him to live

out of the air, out hanging with Pynchon
in Ithaca, boozing with Fariña,
flooring it on a loose-change Odyssey
with a physics professor's daughter, a siren

named Mary you'll track down if living, if she's
still sane. We climb the Pyramid of the Sun,
the roof of Teotihuacán,
and as I'm listening my heart goes

out to you, my son-in-law whom I love,
whose father I need never be, being no
Odysseus. Thank the gods in Florida
my own father's there, *all* there, living the life

every retired hero deserves to lead—
stone crab, high cholesterol, and a woman
loving, faithful. Luck. Some get chosen human
sacrifices, hearts going out to feed

the gods, who'll thank the desert with rain. Now
together we stand atop. I'm out of breath.
I gulp thin air and sneak your photograph
against the ghost city where once lived two

hundred thousand, who constructed this mountain
among the sacred mountains. In the clouds
Quetzalcoatl and all the serpent-gods
burn up, ignited in the falling sun.

IXCUINTLI

The national dog
of Mexico,
hairless save
for a tuft on top,
curly toupée
or stiff gray Mohawk,
stands its ground
and won't yield.
Rufino Tamayo
painted its jaws
dwarfing its body,
blood-blind eyes
and flame-lined teeth,
a dog of war,
dog of the earth.
So rare now that
a cadre kept by
Dolores Olmedo,
Rivera's now-
ancient patron,
constitute
a curiosity
tourists poke
at through the fence,
they descend
from long before
history, white
history, wild
things made pets
and food by vanished
peoples, say,
the Colima of
the Pacific Coast
who did not worship
these rather un-
prepossessing creatures
yet loved them and so

fashioned terra
cotta dogs,
dogs eating
corn, dogs
eating rats,
dogs growling,
but also dogs poised
to lick your
hand, even
pairs of dogs
bluntly upright in a
kind of dance,
teeth bared, the clay
incised to hint at
wrinkles round the eyes,
their blunt ears
alert, their little
potbellies
perfectly pudgy,
figures found
in deep Colima
tombs meters
underground,
companions for
the postlife trip,
the soul's shepherds,
worriers of
the spirits,
friends fearless
of the airless
world, small certain
teeth eternally
ready.

THE GUY WHO PASSED ME DOING 90 MPH AND PLAYING THE TRUMPET

For David H. Porter

Left hand in charge of steering, his right on his
valves, lips compressed—jeez, how could his embouchure
hold firm in thruway traffic?—why this
lunatic didn't create fresh carnage

beats me; the speeding jerks on their yammering
cell phones lead sainted lives by comparison.
I love that blessed solitude while
driving, that heavenly, insulated

half-hour or so so quiet except for my
car wheels revolving, turning the world under-
foot. Cool and modern, hot, baroque, or
classical? Armstrong or Miles or Purcell?

So What? or Copland's *Fanfare*? Or *Taps* for those
cut down like grain as Gabriel harvests his
highway? Yes, *Taps* for everybody
jamming the planet, those half a dozen

more hornmen blowing up the proverbial
storm, burning ancient charts in a riff like an
X-ray whose tonic revelation
rouses the dead to the flame of sunrise.

TEMPERA

Explosions bloomed everywhere after
the autumn fireball, the skyscraper
unzipping. Forsythia flamed
through the neighbors' fence and consumed
the pickets. This morning, the egg
I dropped stared sullenly back,
its primordial tempera
smashed to raw glue on the ground,
the yolk that could feed and fix the world,
that medium for Gentile's
and Simone's miracles,
the Magi with their camels, Mary
who with just an egg made history.

2
IN CAMERA

MYSTERIES

Trompe l'oeil triumphant! The architectural
details, the loud Greek key frieze like a maze,
the cool egg-and-dart molding—sleights of space
that make my fingers ache to caress the wall

from yards away, behind the rusting chain.
And yet the frescoed humans register
flat—not all human: brandishing a mirror
a putto waggling wings that look strapped on

clenches crossed legs as if he needs to potty
while the maidservant studying his glass,
performing sacred rituals of dress,
prepares to bind the gold hair of her lady.

Putto and maid look comfortably immured:
nothing they do demands a third dimension;
it's mystifying how little illusion
the painter mustered in a town this cultured,

this sophisticated. Even the matron—
sposa—even the lady has been partly
rendered to provoke shudders: see that clumsy
wrist, how her bent little finger looks broken

and her yellow gown cascades irrespective
of her lower anatomical dimensions.
Yet in the teeth of such incompetence,
in this remarkably uncontemplative

ritual of the morning, she has paused,
half her hair held high upon her head
awaiting the supple fingers of her maid,
to stare at us. It's the first time she has gazed

out from the wall, and on fresh mystery
outside her glass she's fixed her long-dead eyes.

The world's the mirror where we return her gaze,
stunned by the painter's sudden mastery:

her upper arms' ingratiating flesh,
the gauzy nothing of her dress's bodice
which can't conceal a candid breast, unless
it's damage from the baptism of ash

that kept us strangers eighteen centuries.
Above her head, the key-frieze yields to crumbling
plaster; below, a line where the earth's trembling
fractured her clavicle. Her curious

expression, calm in its calamity,
with full-fleshed lips immobile as her heart,
cracks no codes, whispers no nothings about art,
wearing the long fault of mortality.

FLOPPING THE NEGATIVE

Everything looks so casual
   we should know better:
      the book fallen
      open at the just-legible line,
the lilies holding their breath in the crystal
   vase, the chamber
        pot with its blue Hebrew
as if stumbled on at a Temple
jumble sale,
        the Virgin's blue
     velvet gown
       hushed lushly in apprehension,
         and the shockingly red
         clothes and curtains of the bed
     guilelessly inviting us, weary with old sensation,
     while blaring their alarm. Even
Gabriel
       in full rainbow
   feather
     looks as though he's just popped in
off some celestial
   street. Every letter
     of his salutation,
       his ripe *Ave,*
   dangles like a fruit in the succulent air.
     Yet we've dropped in

on history: her words,
the world-changing words
   wing thick through the painted space
   upside-down as
   if burned upon our retinas,
and backwards,
     traveling from Mary back up,
       whistling past the ear of the angel
         fast as any dove and burnished
     as in a daguerreotype.

> The blazingly palpable
> world stands
> forever reversed:
> *all hail*
> *fallen Eva*—a new chance
> to make it dazzle,
> to get it right before our eyes.
> We recognize
> in this lushly furnished
> chamber, this camera of cameras,
> a place
> almost for us, for every species,
> conceived by this frightened, pious
> and calm girl—
> hands crossed
> like wings upon her breast—
> untouched,
> available,
> almost every girl,
> almost for the birds.

FLEMISH ADORATIONS

I love to worship women in the markets
evaluating ducks and lop-eared rabbits
or gossiping atop skinny stone bridges
that step over the toy canals of Bruges.
Straight dogmatic noses guide us, never
in the air but down to earth, to their
open lips pouting, round on each small mouth,
the world hanging on every word they breathe.
For they are Mary, wresting everlasting
handmaidenship from Jan van Eyck or Memling,
women we have loved for centuries,
pursued once in chapels and dark chantries
and now museums, objects of meditation
what with their pale foreheads, pearly dentition,
and hair cascading in rapid copper rivers,
the daughters of the daughters of the daughters
whose frank faces kept painters sleepless. Heaven,
their altos sing, looks like nothing we love in
the universe so much as our own world:
it's nowhere, the artists know, but here, peopled
with such extraordinary specimens
throughout the agora, snug in their jeans,
not the sumptuous velvet robes whose lacing
educates the palate to fetishizing.
Under the moist, phlegmatic Flemish sun
a glazed clarity glowing through their skin
sets off the marketplace's flood of squawks,
the ducks, chickens, and krumhorn Flemish that strikes
me stupid, like great music. I stand dumb,
a lucky votary in a museum
whose painted women nurse immortal sons
between shifts at the mussel restaurants,
the single mothers, inaccessible
mammals ministering to my table.

LOOKING OUT

I open the box of shades, these glossy leaves drained
of life, to guide
   your photo up, my monochrome
      Eurydice.
From your white windowframe
you study this living room,
     a teenaged scientist,
    evidence swirling before you
   condensing into a new
     cosmos. In the past
you wonder at this bald head,
      the phenomenon
        of color,
      and just what power
has plucked you from your underworld.
        Love
   doesn't occur to you.
       The future
        rides on your adolescent armor:
    your serious yet almost
       smirking stare,
     the silly ribbon
       struggling in your hair.
  Silvery emblem,
         uniquely positive
      document of your teen-
  aged face, hardly
  art, hardly
       life—
  ghost with a gleam,
shade
        in your fifteenth year,
       forgive
   my averting my
      gaze in favor of
     your fleshly heir

and lowering you once more to your dark bed,
      your chaste
  dream
              of the fulfilled life
     you cannot know
       you haven't missed.

A SNAPSHOT IS A MOMENT'S MONUMENT

It's all and not enough
holding you in my hand,
a piece of contraband
smuggled out of life:
this ancient photograph,
a bough, a magic wand,
a passport to a land
that moves me and can't move.

Can I rendezvous closer
with your teenaged face,
your smart mouth that displays
a fresh smirk for your father
who spirits away your picture,
who's docked you in this pose
with sun dazzling your eyes?
Now smile—hold it—forever—

and here in a medium shot
your cardigan, white blouse,
and smile strain to disguise
desire lumped in your throat
thick as the muffler's knot
an anxious mother ties
to guard against your loss.
Relic of spent light,

adolescent ghost,
pale diamond that can cut
a heart or monument,
a shutter claps the past
behind your mouth's sly twist,
fleshly and celibate.
Holy counterfeit,
icon fresh as lust,

how can I understand
you standing in my hand?

FIFTEEN

In 1962 the sun reflects
brilliantly off the sandstone wall. You stand
outside your school. The assistant principal,
your father, focuses and snaps the shutter.
The shadow cast on the wall is his shadow.
You stare into the sun. You are fifteen

and flash a look as though you've spent all fifteen
years posing for his inexpensive reflex
camera, with your father's cool, focused shadow
creeping closer. You cannot understand
why every year this pressing of the shutter
obsesses him, as though his principal

design were to detain you (his principal
demands this week's detention figures) fifteen
minutes while fumbling the focus and shutter
speed. The living lens of your eye reflects
the world in miniature: I see him stand,
before he cast a far gaunter shadow,

hovering in a blue suit, the mortal shadow
of Prospero, an assistant principal
nailing the Caliban who set the grandstand
fire. You, Miranda, stand unkissed. The fifteen-
cent button popped from your cardigan reflects
a watchful frugality that makes me shudder.

Tonight, your folks at bridge, you'll bang the shutter,
carefully paint with lipstick and eyeshadow,
and dream wide-eyed a bedroom that reflects
worldly perfection, the passionate principle
of light in jewels and water in the fifteenth
century. The Arnolfinis stand

staring out, red bed ready to withstand
their homely devotions. Van Eyck clicks the shutter,

their convex mirror contracting him, fifteen
feet away, into a lazuli shadow
sanctioning erotic joy, the principal
business of marriage. Northern sun reflects

off oranges that stand guard in the shadow.
The shutter leaks light, and our principal
witness, your fifteen-year-old eye, reflects.

SHADOW

Some shadows look so dark, so luscious and desirable
   light
can't be responsible.
      Across the border we find ourselves
      under a foreign law of shadow
      articulate as in old photographs,
   that harsh black and white
        world that stings our eyes
   and brings balm. Light
        was made for darkness.
Life takes its toll,
   we ferry ourselves
      across, we draw
      conclusions, we draw
        to a close,
      draw

the shutter. Everyone
   casts a shadow,
      save in this photograph
where you cast none
   on the glass doors behind you.
You're fifteen
      and your lips rise to a laugh,
while on the sandstone
   wall beside you,
   angled like a spy,
   an eavesdropping shadow
      betrays an interest. It's enough

to make me shudder,
someone waltzing over
   my grave. I want to cast
that shadow: not you but your father
the photographer
clicking the shutter,
      an attempt like Joshua's

                to freeze the sun,
                    to focus
                        entirely on you here and now
(there
            then).
                I focus on your face
        to shut up the shadowy past
away on charmed paper
            slumbering in its dark box, awaiting light's buzz.
        I am the shadow your father cast
                decades ago
to snap your determined stare,
            to seize the sun
with a single finger
        opaque against it, to immortalize
                your face
                your face that launches us
            into the shadows.

CAPTIVITY IN SPRING

The robin's cyclical ruckus,
its helical whistle
like a spiraling molecule,
tenses in spring to knock us
out of our jeans. Gets hard to focus

on the world at hand—rather,
in my hand: old photograph
that captures half your life
for me, fixed by the shutter—
click—you're now fifteen, before

the correct blocks of your school,
before a quarter century
unspools, replicated like the rusty
gate of the blue jay's bray
now topping the robin's wrangle.

The coils, the toils, the zippers
of our years spirit us into shadow.
Well. Let us consult in camera.
Music, birdies. Be we prisoners?
Enter in bravely; clap to the shutters.

NETHER STOWEY

Dear Coleridge, I'm a stranger in your house
and do not think of you as lunatic
or some nut nodding off to opium,
but a man feeling too keenly the touch
of other human beings, who needed air,
cold air around him to anesthetize
his overloaded senses just enough
to get on with the grim business of living.
I'm shivering to be breathing in your parlor,
this small room where, sitting in colloquy
with birds singing bower songs, leaves blazing, ice
lengthening in the winter moonlight, you
all conspired to bless your son, sleeping,
inexplicable as a foreign land,
love offering the principle of translation.
The sad past melts away in the sublime
cold. Dorothy tells how you walked the knife-edge
of Helvellyn—on either side a sheer
drop—at night, in shoes with licorice soles.
In childlessness I hear your pen enact
those words—*My babe so beautiful*—scratching
the midnight silence like a record groove's
promise of Mozart. The missing film
that fluttered on your fire I've loaded in
my camera, the little chamber I use
to violate your intimacy. Make me
a companionable form. As much
a stranger as on barging in, I steal
away hearing your strange nocturnal words
collect, turning my head sadder, stranger still.

JANE AUSTEN, INVENTOR OF BASEBALL

> . . . it was not very wonderful that Catherine, who had by nature nothing heroic about her, should prefer cricket, baseball, riding on horseback, and running about the country at the age of fourteen, to books. . . .
>
> *Northanger Abbey*

How to learn the signs, how to decide
to commit, how to know mere manners from
true ardor, how to take a pitch, how
to hang in, how to foul off Wickham's trick
deliveries, how to connect with Darcy's
devastating curve or Mr. Knightley's
high hard one, how to dust yourself off from
a brushback, how to read the rules to your
advantage, how to plot a strategy,
how to work out the crucial late walk under
fading light with the moon rising over
the fence and nightingales singing their anthem,
how to protect your lead, how to hit
and run, how to rally when visitors
keep chipping away, how to play defense,
how to guard against the steal, when to play
for one and when to try for two, when
to sacrifice, how to negotiate
long-term contracts, how to determine if
and when it's safe to come home, how to read.

CHAWTON

Ms. Austen, I'm past your age when you died
and where are my six delightful novels,
four of them masterpieces? So I wander
through your last house, rather gaga you
could read the world the way we must read *Emma,*
ears pricked by the overemphatic rattle
of a teacup, sniffing the subtle shift
of molecules aloft in drawing rooms,
the rancidness of condescension souring
the clear ozone of magnanimity,
recording the flirtatious rustle of
a sleeve or cuff: an art of innuendo,
of chances mostly missed, of hems muddied,
of half-smiles and raised eyebrows flat ignored—
a world where *everyone* is always reading.
You permit us, rarely, the second chance
to put things back, to get them right, and, more
rarely, that mystical phenomenon
marital bliss, the happy creatures fruitful
in the garden with serpents nipping at
their ankles futilely. In the drawing room
bent over your small round table, you write
a firm deliberate script apparent as
daylight, as blunt as Darcy, a hand so clear
it harbors you in every loop and whorl,
sheltering you inside your woman's work:
the mystery of Life itself (so much
for Mary Shelley!) from nothing, from air
and ink, while eavesdropping for footsteps on
the stair, the flinging of the listening door
that makes the whole world disappear beneath
a blotter or inside a folio.
Your roses and snapdragons chuckle out
in the garden; you're working on *Persuasion;*
I turn the doorknob, dying to catch you,
but the hinge squeals and you're no longer there.

ABSORPTION

Stare at a color till you become the color
and red fields with fiery barriers surround you.
Painting absorbs you, and your world grows fuller.

The canvas reaches out to you. Get closer,
drink from deep reservoirs designed to drown you:
stare down that color, dare become that color

clutching you, turning your eyesight duller.
Faint green ghosts wrangling in the red confound you,
the paint absorbing you, your world grown fuller,

flusher, the canvas raving like a lover
whose words knock in your head. Without a sound you
stare at a color till you become the color.

Now take these late blues, deep blacks, and discover
your cheek not dark but drained. Put it down to
painting absorbing your life, growing fuller

of every shade, abandoning you to pallor
yet reaching from an absence so profound you
stare at its color till you become—no color.
Paintings absorb you, and their life grows fuller.

IN HIDING

They've ferreted out an angle
in the great green garden,
assuming its geometry
to hide from the angel
or minister calling
in that black bullhorn basso.
The stern hand of heaven
is loving as a tree
whose blushing has begun,
its shameful leaves falling.

He once stood guard personally,
kapo of the compound,
waggling a father's finger.
Cruel trials of surgery;
nightmares for anesthetic.
Experiments no longer.
He's withdrawn. Clouds abound,
through which his fluids water
a thirsty firmament.
Eden has shrunk.

Adam and Eve crouch
cold as amphibians,
though Adam's thickened thigh
and the fulcrum of his crotch
attest he's no frog
with a jewel behind his brow:
the trembling of his leg's veins,
the twitching of his eye.
Eve lays her arm on Adam's
like fuel, log on log.

What price for knowledge
cruel as the grave
and cunning as ripe fruit?

Harvest is luscious carnage,
cloying but spurring our wants,
a dull thud at the heart
stupid as a knife
sawing a tree at the root.
We kill ourselves for love
and eat the evidence.

Eve shields her virginal face
from the gnostic radiance.
Her palms are scored with lines
like a chimpanzee's;
her twisted mouth cries *Stop*.
In the passionate embrace
of the fatherland they squeeze
into their coffin space
behind some barbarous trees.
In time they will burn up.

ICONOGRAPHY

Kneeling on the crossbar
Eve offers a skull
to a bewildered Adam.
Never seen that before!
What happened to the apple?
Exposing her pudendum

to Adam, who reclines
with his skinny arms
crossed over his crotch,
she aims to tease his bones,
to straighten him out. He dreams
far to the west a church

where a lamb sits reading a book.
He dreams off in the east,
its oil lost down a hole,
a sinister synagogue.
A hammer in a fist
threatens a sinner's skull,

through whose eyes the snake
slinks like a chromosome.
The apple's in its jaws!
But the skull's jaws will not speak,
this skeleton of our Adam
grinning at the cross.

ADORATION

From the farthest reaches of the altar
through the craggy rock walls of the landscape
of crumpled brown craft paper, its geologic
folds, its electric fountains replenishing
themselves continuously, a procession
winds through the perils of the Holy Land,
far beneath the stuccoed dome or vault
of every parish church in Mexico.
The camels, burros, and turkeys, the peasants,
the magi and the mariachi bands
negotiate the rumpling countryside
to the grand brown paper cave to worship
baby *Jesús,* who finds himself surrounded
by shepherds, well-dressed bourgeois citizens,
the ox and ass of course, flocks of sheep, even
puppies, kitty cats, and armadillos.
Mary and Joseph clearly were expecting
the world and the welcome mat is out: they've strung
a thousand twinkling lights from the humble cave
out to the hinterlands for *Navidad,*
designed to catch the eye of all wayfarers
as if a star igniting out of nowhere
might provide uncertain illumination
or prove a conjugal hallucination.

JUST SAY THE WORD

Say the secret Word
   and win fifty dollars.
      But in this snapshot
      you're silent as art:
no finger censors
      your rubicund lip,
no goony bird
   hovers
       pregnant with heavenly gossip,
     no book cracked flat
        spreadeagled at the tattling line.
Word unheard,
      Word unseen.

Incommunicado?
   Pondering in your heart?
     Ripe
    Latin fat
with gesso
       hangs palpable in the air
of the miraculous fresco
at Santissima Annunziata,
      cramming Mary's ear
   in letters thick as alphabet
        blocks, yet spreading such serenity
         across her trecento face
        that as she crosses
        hands on her breast you can *see*
        her *Ecce ancilla domini*
       galumphing through the ether—
backwards and up-

side down,
   a pregnant Word a flesh-
    ly Word a Word
       that'll tumble you for the money

                that'll give you a roll in the hay.
    The world
            hinges
on such encounters, and doesn't the congregation
                know it! Ancient women in black
                who ache
for the Virgin's crown,
        and, brows yet unfurrowed,
                swishing their cotton dresses,
    pious girls spread throughout the church
like a Tuscan field anticipating grain.
                Shall Gabriel
                smile on them all?

Just *say* it:
    Word like a Big Bang,
the hirsute
        backdoor birds
                singing a streak
    bluer than any human tongue
you bet
                your life on
                it, nightingale's liquid insinuation
            gone lewd as a squawk,
        a private body of words
    invisibly strung
                in a grammar
                more vulgar
you bet
                than any Latin.

STILL LIFE

Farewell, said our ancient ancestors,
   great snails and ammonites
     who before they vanished
turned photographers,
leaving us pictures,
      posing themselves
        in darkness, in mud.
Pelographers,
      then. Their prints were negatives,
fixed in ocean floors,
   fleshed
        out with layer on layer
     of mud.
Elegant forebears
     who whirled their world
     from themselves,
        their muscular shimmer
  went dust, and their breathtaking self-portraits
    ended up astonished—
      still lifes.

Daguerre knew people
couldn't keep as still,
   endless minutes before his lens,
     so first he shot sculpture,
  humans
     fulfilled
in slower stone. Next, he posed his prize fossil
   shelves: stone scallop fans,
   fat unicorn-horn whelks, coral brains,
       mute cornucopiae
        of snails and nautili,
      spirals forever stilled
   on silver.

You can't deny death
   its solemn beauty, the stark

          lesson in swoony vanitas
                Daguerre's fossil
     rack
                   left behind. Yet tip
                   the daguerreotype
 in the light, bathe
              it in dazzle,
           and the stone creatures
 breathe,

 a resurrection served on a silver plate.
     Now let us savor
          our dead:
     fossils. Or grandmother with silver
             hair and skin, a silver shadow
                   tarnishing her arm.
     We gather
           family upon family
                to squeeze into our wooden frame
                   urgently, becoming specimens
     for a dusty shelf. Mother's hand smoothing our hair,
                   father's stony expirations,
                   a cousin's
                   clammy kiss, the summons
         from the hooded
     photographer,
 and we freeze, stop breathing, and commit
       our bodies (it's the life) to picture after picture.

IN CAMERA

Eternal life via a hinged wood box,
   a silvered plate, a man drunk
   on the stink
      of visionary chemicals:
         pneumonia, scarlet fever, a rheumatic
heart, anything plucks
       off a child of nine, leaving a thick
         Victorian glaze
      on its eyes,
   a bruise where its skull's
         been passionately kissed,
          a body perfectly composed
       for worship on the settee, no nervous tic
  or blink
      to blur the work
         of the daguerreotypist
aiming forever to fix
        nature
        here in the parlor.

Light's remains absorb us. Whatever reflects
   can illuminate
     the silver buried
deep in a dark box,
   sun banging on metal, a sleight
     to gong the spirit
back to our world, where artifacts
      (this corpse's dazzling image, ferried
        to new life in the palm)
          can, after full immersion
         in poison,
       thrive in a wood frame,
     a cold child offered
on a cold, reflective plate.

From your frame
  on the piano

           you smile, Father,
       as if you didn't know
             a grimmer image knocks
             in my mind's dark box—
       a grayer picture,
    your face grisaille as old snow
 into which your headlong frame,
             like a filthy joke,
       a pratfall at a formal dinner,
             lurched prone
                   and made a last impression.
       Neither gin nor
             formaldehyde, not even
             the polished, hand-joined oak
    coffin's casement window
       from which you cast your
             frozen last look,
             could put the trick
                   across, the bright illusion
 you were at rest, or warm.

THE GOLDEN CHAMBER

They found the girls buried
outside Cologne, creating
a sensation. Before long
strange stories spread.
Of course they were girls
no longer but skulls and sticks,
flesh, gowns, and curls
long dust by 1106.
A slipped pen in translation
confirmed St. Ursula
and her eleven thousand
sister virgin martyrs
breasted the Rhine in eleven ships
to be slaughtered by
poleaxe, sword, crossbow,
faint smiles and the kiss
of Christ upon their lips.
Eleven thousand virgins
yield a lot of bones;
The newfound martyr lode
(though many bones were men's)
boomed the relic trade
yet piled up many a cartload
to stock St. Ursula's shrine.

How do you articulate
the bones of eleven
thousand skeletons?
A scapula can't recite
whose shoulder fleshed it once;
even skulls with jaws
keep silent intercourse.
A mystic had a vision
of virgins by the dozen,
each floating from the mist

to offer up her name,
but none published a claim
for her kneecap, rib, or wrist.

The head's a reliquary
for the skull, the skull
for the brain. Artisans
carved elegant wooden
reliquary busts
to snug the unfleshed
crania: young women
born of the cut live tree,
modeled on the living
daughters of Cologne,
their delicate wood hair
curling like the Rhine
framing painted faces
we might mistake for angels',
betraying subtle smiles
as if a virgin's innocence
housed the hoariest knowing,
the way the softest skin
provides a smooth disguise
for understanding bone.
On the Feast of St. Ursula,
October 21st,
the daughters of Cologne
would each take up a bust
to carry around the church
and out through all the town,
hundreds of murdered virgins
miraculously reborn,
the same golden dresses
and wise, shy smiles,
the same gold tresses,
the same violent Rhine.

And the wooden girls return
to their ornate gold niches
in the Golden Chamber
where today their smiles burn
a hole in the heart like a small
death. The upper
walls of the gold room glitter
with rustic herringbone stick
patterns as on Adirondack
great camp friezes.
Then the illumination:
they're bones, thousands of bones
horizontal, upright,
slanted, stacked, piled,
sorted by shape and size,
tibia, fibula, rib,
the bones of hundreds of virgins
raised to ornament
this gilt and gruesome bower,
a grand memento mori,
a golden charnel house
bequeathing us a foretaste,
bones blissfully composed,
articulate at last,
chanting a cappella,
spelling VRSVLA.

3
INEVITABLE

MENNONITES BY THE SEA

Those nearly naked sauntering by, breasts
bikinied and buttocks thonged, rolling along
beneath white dazzle, before the turquoise sea,
their moist, sun-venomed fascination—vanished.
More than the dolphin leaping fifty yards
from shore, a group of women has swept me
off to the elemental realm of Homer:
not Nausicaa and pals tossing their beach ball,
but something homelier, the world of Winslow,
at once boldly and shyly American.
Mist rises from the sea around these barefoot
six in their brown, black, slate blue, wholesome gray
ankle-length frocks, sedately bobbling, pigeons
among the jungle flock, their tresses tucked
in tight white muslin caps with strings dangling
in the sole gesture of devil-may-care.
The youngest of them runs along the beach,
hair unbonneted, bunched in a white scrunchie.
She teases her bearded father in his homespun
trousers and suspenders, his boots redeeming
him from the burning sand, his broad-brimmed hat
staving off the classical sun. The sea
kisses the women's hems, infusing their
skirts with its brackish solution. They enter
a step, a step further, the ocean spanking
their dresses against their limbs, unexposed
and pale, until the fabric snaps like spandex
on a hip-hop siren, or Nefertiti's
splashy wrappings. How deep will they wade in?
They wear their dresses as the fish wear water,
as if no one were watching, no one lying
nearly naked and nearly unashamed.

A BREAKDOWN

A. R. Ammons, 1926–2001

Coming from anywhere, your poems, they traveled
anywhere, rucksack on the back, hitching
up dungarees, hitching a ride, sentencing
down the road, letting their hair down, letting
themselves tumble down scroll-like and pushing
their lines through all those colons, never flinching
from all the nonsense we push through our colons,
compost being our biodegradable
identity, giving away the game,
giving off heady perfumes, signaling
hey, all the crap we spin out of ourselves:
haute cuisine for someone else, a fly, say, or
bacteria, imagination just
another enzyme, how the whole damned process
of breaking down never breaks down, whoa, never
ends, only that in the localest terms
we end, ending up brokedown into spelling
and if we're lucky intimations of
some glory and some end that we use to
distract us from that glory and that end.

SUCH STUFF

    Charles LeDray, *Tower*

A high stool perches on a Rietveld chair.
The Rietveld sits upon a Shaker table,
the table straddles
the ridge of a little house
that rests upon a chest
of drawers supported by
another chair, another table, on down to
the stepladder, the sideboard, the great sprawling desk,
and the wheelbarrow leaned against
an antique bedstead stood
on its head—the world piled up on this precarious
three-foot tower the sculptor
carved, the label says,

from human bone.

How could anything human take
in hand a just-cold human rib,
put its mortal architecture to the knife,
and whittle into virtual
life a ghost-chair from this scrap of perfect spiral
that guarded a heart?

Is everything material?

One man's mate had been his bone,
such stuff, still-
warm, fashioned into flesh,
black hair and an insatiable
instinct for fruit and information.

Thanks be to knowledge, the canker,
the drop of vinegar we might not notice
corrupting the wine. Thanks to the curator,
we know our medium,

the assembly of our clean, cruel furniture
into the strange
balance that maintains us staring
speechless on this brittle, beautiful tower.

DEATH'S SUIT

An ivory in Munich

Death's double backbone
grants articulation,
the eloquent stacked key-
board of his vertebrae
enabling him to kneel
before the virginal
young woman whose bare breast
and buttocks shiver exposed
despite her desperate
winding of a sheet
from her head down over
her trembling shoulder,
around her back and across
her equally quivering crotch.
His emptied eyes blow
her icy; she's a statue
Death longs to call *Frau:*
with a diadem in her hair
and a pillow beneath her bare
feet, she's a birthday gift
for the cool usurper of birth,
the gutless one who fails
to engage her far-off eyes
that cannot see him kneel,
toad squatting on his tail,
lizard on his kneecap.
He proposes worship
with the carved crucifix
he waggles at her sex,
as if Mary bore her child
and watched him thorned and nailed
to service all the world,
a naked sacrilege
sprung from a naked ribcage.
The flesh-dressed second spine

snakes throughout Death's bone,
popping through the clavicle
to offer her an apple.
Down below, its rattle
shakes its reptilian genius
stiffly from Death's pelvis.
The serpent clamps its jaws
deep in the apple flesh
while she composes a frigid
bridal response to his rigid
suit. Winding herself in
that ignorance of linen
and playing blind,
she will not understand
the snugness of their room
fragrant with balm and loam
till he cakewalks her home
to undertake, her groom.

THE COLLAPSE

The snow ganged up in March
on the roof and around the walls
of our summer cabin,
an old ramshackle Sears
catalog design.
It proved the finishing touch,

for while it was wombed in snow
the cabin could enjoy
something it never dared dream:
structural integrity,
red walls like an ancient tomb
stowed in a white barrow.

The field mice scurried and pissed
and gnawed toothpaste and soap.
The mute typewriter sat stiff
and composed; come thaw its type
would rust. The upright, tone-deaf,
froze out Gershwin and Liszt.

Late in its term, the snow
in the sun's lengthening flame
relaxed its crystal flesh,
tormenting the cabin's frame.
The roof knelt in the slush;
the modular walls fought free,

a leisurely explosion
we found Memorial Day.
The floor entertained the roof;
the six-foot sections lay
spreadeagled on the earth,
none of the windows broken.

BAR MITZVAH IN PRAGUE

The quiz kid on the bimah snatched at Hebrew
falling through the synagogue from the rabbi's
throat, the studied sentences dry as Sinai.
A blue suit snugged him like a carapace

while Moses moseyed a nervous progress through
the mountain's maze, a paradise of thorns.
Down the street the tomb of Rabbi Löw
intoned among the cascading gravestones.

The balcony where Kafka's mother sat
kvelling vibrated with her in female
mystery, an invisible downward float
aromatic and inaccessible;

still higher, from the Gothic attic, Kafka
heard the Golem's whisper like the creaking
of earth, an elemental prayer that Yahweh
let Yossel out to play with the other children.

Breath animated Adam. Some parts of speech
can build new worlds if dropped into the one
blank cranny in the universe, an arch
awaiting the aplomb of its keystone.

The bar mitzvah boy conjured up the stone
tablets Moses smashed and the Israelite
orgy round the calf; soon he'd add his own
gold nib inditing in the shining night,

lit by the frigid flame of father love
breaking out in the Altneushul that day:
Blessed be he who has relieved me of
all responsibility for this boy.

CARMELITE CONVENT, MEXICO DF

Past portraits of sedate saints
at desks like grade school principals,
past dormitory cells where nuns
once whispered prayers to iron bells,
then sank to wooden biers and slept,
we descended to the crypt.

This death-intoxicated land
gives skeletons the final chuckle.
They play in a mariachi band,
hack a laptop, dance flamenco,
sing a feather boa torchsong,
soar on batwings, fish, go drinking—

Death makes mirth in Mexico.
The jawbones slacken in a laugh,
the lively, eyeless sockets know
nothing ends in an epitaph,
for pleasure lies in getting stripped
of everything. Then, in the crypt,

the glass-topped coffins let us view
the corpses of some denizens
of a colonial century,
some of abbots, some of nuns,
others sporting finer dress,
all whitened by the same distress.

A person often mummifies
in the capital's sapless climate.
Though ancient gum sealed one nun's eyes,
some woolen and some fleshly habit
had worn away. Thus she gave us
a peekaboo flash of naked pelvis.

Others suffered harder wear,
ribs poking out between the buttons,

their boots, sewn of the supplest leather
for bourgeois metatarsal bones,
each now clumsily damned to dangle
from the slenderest, whitest ankle.

We couldn't say they lay at rest
because the mummied mouths stood open
with this or that peculiar twist
as if their maiden glimpse of heaven
contradicted what they'd heard.
Every body looked appalled

on death—or the death of an illusion—
though one skull, maybe once a lawyer,
grinned with clean white satisfaction
atop his once-tight, boiled wool collar
grown ample, the kid glove on his fist
skinned back to bare a knuckled wrist.

MEMORIAL CHAPEL

We've arrived expressly to be transported
while we sit stock-still in the college chapel's
1800 Federal architecture,
    witnessing music,

Schubert, Bach, Prokofiev, Shostakovich,
week in, week out, making this room a spare, sparse
paradise, a garden where sound waves loiter
    rounded to crystal.

Now, for instance, Beethoven's Grosse Fuge in
B-flat major scrolls from the quartet's guts while
listening I study again the names carved
    back of the players,

marble-clad memorial to the Great War
dead, the undergrads and alumni who got
butchered giving Europe democracy it
    didn't desire and

lie transported off overseas. The Grosse
Fuge spreads thick, deciduous layers, aural
flavors—ash, ambrosia—in living ears un-
    stopped with the earth, un-

like the ears of Wesley D. Karker, Luther
Hagar, William W. Waiteskill, Herbert
Rankin, Talbot Carmichael, Allen Ashton,
    Kennedy Conklin,

Wolcott Caulkins, Alwyn G. Levy, Howard Thorne, and
dozens more stone deaf to the music, deafer
than a post, than Beethoven, college guys now
    deafer than when they

   sat in boring lectures and dreamt that bloody
   high romance, imagined those French *jeunes filles,* but
   found nothing transporting them, no returning
      even as cargo.

THE HILDESHEIM DOORS

And here I'm sitting on a low stone bench,
but not a bench, I see now—it's a wall,
an old foundation round a grassy patch
whose center, a six-pointed memorial,

marks where the fringes brushed the parchment scrolls,
then blessed the lips, letting glad voices sing
the Flood, the flames of Sodom, chariot wheels
sunk in the sea, the fleshy reveling

around the Golden Calf. Half Hildesheim
got flattened by the Allies in '45,
plane following plane, bomb following holy bomb,
mere weeks before Red tanks inspired the love-

death in the bunker. In the marketplace
Hildesheim's good burghers schemed to rebuild,
timber by half-timber, in full Renaissance
variegated splendor, the butchers' guild,

a charming resurrection, and so clean
you'd expect the master butcher to be Mickey,
chauffeured by Goofy decked in lederhosen.
But it's for real, bearing out the lucky

destiny of a city that embraces
its own terrible role in history.
In the southern quarter a host of houses
survived the bombs, their sixteenth-century

frames jauntily crooked, plaster walls whitewashed
spanking clean. Just one building went to rubble,
this synagogue, burned down on Kristallnacht.
It's easier to make a memorial

of something that's no longer necessary.
At Hildesheim cathedral, great bronze doors

one thousand years old spin out the twinned story
of fall and redemption, of fruitful loss

and bloody victory. Their style shocks us.
It's frighteningly modern: Adam and Eve
fling spindly limbs over their nakedness
beneath the blasted prehistoric tree,

their fingers pointing everywhere to stain
anyone but themselves. They know. That serpent
curling among the flowers like a vine
has lost his voice and can't plead innocent.

Their round mouths wail in cartoon disbelief
at the rough justice of their sentence, numbered
from Day One. Moony heads smooth as if new-shaved,
plucked out for shunting down a ramp, they're tumbled

toward death—for stealing fruit! sun-ripe and warm;
we bear helpless witness. Smiling in wait,
wearing his dark suit like a uniform,
the sexton flips a switch. The lights black out

and brother kills brother under an eclipse
worthy of a crucifixion. No angel's
words to Mary, burning through space from lips
to virgin ear, can light these bronze rectangles

chock-full of God's love, each comic strip panel
a boxcar coupled on a one-way track
to terminal, screaming right on schedule,
rectangle after rectangle in the dark.

THREE WOMEN

    John Currin, *Stamford After-Brunch*

Everyone's head's too big.
Everyone's neck's too long.
Everyone's knees are a bit too sharp.
In every way the painter's judged them wrong.

The upholstered chair crowds the upholstered couch
so the woman at right appears to have one leg
wedged between the furniture. (Ouch.)
But she grins heedlessly, a rich rag,

once a husband's shirt, knotted round her head
in a lusciously careless coiffure,
a round dome palpably echoed
by buttocks that project far past the frame to tender an insolent offer

eluding the eye, embraced by the imagination,
the dirty imagination, the jittery thrill
of this exercise in uncanny titillation.
I adore the beautiful

middle figure, blond hair pulled tight and cascading
around her stretched Bronzino throat, her smile an emblem
of occult delight. She tucks up her too-scrawny right leg
and I can discover her left leg and her right arm

nowhere. Her face betrays a gleam from nowhere,
stupidly brilliant, her serene downcast eyes
almost distracting from how, reckless of nature,
her amazing, realistic eyebrows rise

an inch too high on her forehead's cool slate.
The dark-haired woman at left laughs so hard
she squints, her hand a claw, her upper teeth
glinting in lamplight like a scalpel blade.

Clutching little cigars, martini glasses
chiming in a triad, they enjoy
a cackle at the fruits of happiness.
The room hums homey with conspiracy,

a rumbling hum shuddering safety glass,
scorching books, sparing dental evidence
from blown-up buses, holy sites, whole cities
resurrected picturesque as ruins

in coffeetable books browsed by three women
hot as fore-gossip, cool as an after-whisper,
spinning, shearing, and casting us out to moan
in an envy inevitable as winter.

THE OLD AND NEW CEMETERIES

For Steve Stern

With a slow, silent clatter
like dominoes the stones
spotted with worn Hebrew
clamber over each other
as if they were prisoners
clawing up to air
over the backs of loved ones,
trampling darlings deeper
in the breathless chamber.
The stones can barely stand,
having exhausted underground
by 1792,
when Prague determined to close
this rough medieval ghetto,
the graveyard for Jews,
and dedicate a new.

A Jew goes into the ground
obeying an ancient text.
A Jew must rot in the earth
till the corpse is full perplexed
in one dusty compound.
This the bones comprehend
when newborns first gulp breath,
breath that burns like flame
or soothes the lungs like snow,
breath that begins to blow
through city and tragic wood,
whirling Eve and Adam,
each dustman and bonemaid,
back to their filthy home.
Into the ground they go.

Rabbi Löw's ancient tomb
stands a little aloof,

a crown among snaggled teeth
with a dark plot of gum around it,
a little *Totenraum*.
The rabbi composts beneath,
dutifully confounded
with other human filth.
He'd popped the letter *shin*
into the mouth of his Golem
who roared alive to avenge
Prague's docile Jewry
living among the goyim
as though behind plate glass,
a stone's throw apart,
now suddenly astounded
by their creature's gory rage—
blood for a slaughtered milk
cow or a smashed shopfront—
vicarious fury sprung
from the heart's locked attic,
now loosed from a secret page.

Ages from that neighborhood,
the new graveyard is light
and airy as a park.
Its avenues run straight,
straight stones on every block,
no crowding in shadow,
no camp or Old World ghetto.
At a much-visited corner
lie the bones of Kafka.
Burnt offerings, bric-a-brac,
scrawlings in demotic
American litter the grave,
each Elvis-like devotion
corrupt with naiveté
as if his corpse could hear,

as if the bones could care,
as if they held some truth
to heal the mourner's clay—
the sort of thing to drive
all Kafkas back to bed,
black covers over the head.

In the new cemetery
the empty boulevards stretch
for what seems miles, the sky
the color of sifted ash.
On the wooded alley past Kafka
the graves attain their end;
regardless of command
none comes tumbling after.
The Jews of course went away
on trains propelled by breath,
exhaust from the black earth,
an orderly transportation
no one had foreseen
and none dared prophesy,
only to return
in compounds of their own,
a gray precipitation
weightier than fog,
to other earth than Prague.

POETS' PARK, MEXICO DF

You and I risked our necks to get there, dodging
the mad cars careening around it, merging
from all angles, a condensing asteroid
swarm. Our eyes, forced open, wept in the acrid
air. Breathlessly we landed on that island
green as imagination, nearly blind
to traffic, though we heard the autos grumble.
Throughout this miniature oasis people
strolled, played with their kids, lunched. One couple necked
like no tomorrow near a less romantic
memorial to a poet I'd never heard
of. His bronze head, looking grotesquely severed,
rested on an open concrete book
as if admonishing all poets, "Look
on this life, this work, and think again:
would you choose loving under this lush green
or locking yourself up in an attic room?
The real, polluted thing? Or some daydream?"
We walked arm in arm; head after bronze head
would neither speak nor smile nor grudge a nod.
Exhilaration? Gray contentment? Anguish?
Who knew? I had no syllable of Spanish.
Emerging from the poets' sanctuary,
the car-stink stinging, our eyes again gone blurry,
we found a fountain fashioned like a pen,
its nib replenishing a pool. A fountain-
pen. I pose beside it in your photo,
writing, writing forever with clear water.

www.ingramcontent.com/pod-product-compliance
Lightning Source LLC
Chambersburg PA
CBHW022109160426
43198CB00008B/411